How to Operate a Freelance Writing Business and How to be a Ghostwriter

Insider Secrets from a Professional Ghostwriter Proven Tips and Tricks Every Author Needs to Know About Freelance Writing

Professional Freelance Writer Series #1

Published by The Writing King
www.thewritingking.com

D1496231

How to Operate a Freelance Writing Business and How to be a Ghostwriter

Cover Artist: theamateurzone

Library of Congress Control Number: 2016917209

ASIN: B01EIMN17Y
ISBN: 978-1-943517-53-4 (Paperback)
ISBN: 978-1-943517-61-9 (Hardcover)
ISBN: 978-1-943517-05-3 (eBook)

How to Operate a Freelance Writing Business and How to be a Ghostwriter

Insider Secrets from a Professional Ghostwriter Proven Tips and Tricks Every Author Needs to Know About Freelance Writing

Richard G Lowe, Jr

Table of Contents

Table of Contents i

Introduction...1

Becoming a freelance ghostwriter 3

   What is a ghostwriting project?.....................5

   A successful ghostwriting project..................6

   Agreement 7

   Branding 7

   It is a business 8

Communication is key 11

   Constant communications 11

   Types of communication..............................12

   Email messages 13

   Agendas..14

   Notes 16

   Regular status updates................................17

Getting the business................................19

How much to charge 23

   Pricing formula..25

Statement of work 29

   The basics 30

   Termination..30

   Copyright 31

   Multiple phases...31

   Services not included..................................32

Acknowledgments...32

Writing the book 33
Parts of a book..34

Prerequisites...36

Interviews..36

Research 37

Outline each chapter..38

Doing the writing..38

Revisions 39

After the chapter is accepted 40

Major Revisions...43
Log changes 44

No changes are requested 44

Watch out for changes in scope 45

Changes in scope...47
Minor scope changes..47

changes that result in higher cost.........................48

changes that require expenses 49

Revisiting previously completed work.....................49

All scope changes documented in writing 50

Final revision 51
Edit entire document..52

Completing the project 53
Referral and testimonial.......................................53

Revisions after completion....................................54

Table of Contents

Conclusion..55
About the Author 57

Introduction

So, you think you want to be a freelance ghostwriter? Perhaps you have some writing experience, or you want to earn extra money. Maybe someone asked you to write a book that they want to publish in their own name, or possibly you heard of this thing called ghostwriting, and you want to give it a try.

Ghostwriting is hard work. It is very creative and fulfilling. However, the energy required to peer into a person's mind, read their scrapbooks, make sense of their scribbled notes, and turn all of that into a well-written manuscript is intense.

Being a writer does not mean that you have the tools to be a good ghostwriter. Ghostwriting requires a whole different set of skills on top of writing. You're not creating a book for you; you're writing a book to satisfy the needs and requirements of another person, company, or group. It is a very different thing.

In this book, you will discover the nuts and bolts of ghostwriting and learn how to successfully turn a client's idea into a completed manuscript with the following knowledge:

- ➢ How to manage the process of creating a ghostwritten book from start to finish
- ➢ Written and oral communication skills necessary when interacting with your client
- ➢ What you need to do to gain new ghostwriting business

Introduction

> How to complete a well-written Statement of Work that defines the type of book to be written and how the project will be managed
> How to write the book, one chapter at a time, while utilizing interviews and outlines
> Communicating with your client during the revision process
> Controlling necessary changes—both minor and dramatic—while keeping your project on track
> Delivering your completed manuscript

Ghostwriting is a unique form of writing that, although difficult, can be very rewarding on both a financial and emotional level. I hope you get value from this book and enjoy the adventure of extracting a story from someone's mind and changing it into a completed manuscript.

I hope you enjoy what I've written and find it to be of some value. If you would like to send me a note about this book, feel free to write me at rich@thewritingking.com. If you enjoyed the book, please write a positive review.

Becoming a freelance ghostwriter

I've been a writer since I was a young man. I always enjoyed writing; I like telling a story, and I enjoy passing on the knowledge that I've gained in my life and career. Most of all, I enjoy helping people, and writing is a great way to do that.

When I was in college, I majored in geology, with a minor in English literature. Before the end of my second year, I was offered a job in a startup computer company. I accepted a position as their first application programmer.

Since I could write, I found myself creating letters, proposals, technical documents, user guides, and just about any other written communication required by our various clients. Since my audience was often non-technical in nature, I became very skilled at explaining things without using technical terms.

I continued working in the computer industry, starting as an entry-level programmer and eventually working my way up to Vice President of Consulting. After twelve years working as a consultant, I accepted a position at Trader Joe's as the Director of Computer Operations. During my 33-year career, I wrote over 100 technical documents, and hundreds of articles, proposals, and other shorter works.

Even though I was making a lot of money, my heart told me that I wanted to be a writer. Just before my 20-year anniversary at Trader Joe's, I decided to take an early retirement and begin a writing career. It was time to make my dream come true.

Introduction

My idea was to write those books that I had started but never found the time to complete during my long years working with computers. I had outlines for dozens of novels and several dozen nonfiction books. I had quite a few manuscripts in various stages of completion.

After moving to a new city and settling in, I began to pursue my passion of writing. I decided to start with a series of novels based in a science fiction future. At the same time, I pursued completing about a dozen nonfiction books.

I went to several different writing critique groups each week. In these groups, authors get together, read their works out loud, and provide comments on how to improve each other's manuscripts. I found them very valuable, and my writing skills improved as a result.

I started to pick up freelance ghostwriting projects from these critique groups. Before long, I was busy a good portion of each week interviewing, researching, and writing books for other people.

I quickly discovered that project management skills are critical in a ghostwriting project. In fact, I found that the same skills that I used to manage computer projects—meeting management, outline creation, communication, collaboration, and the production of a Statement of Work—applied directly to freelance writing and ghostwriting books.

I created this book to help writers break into the field of freelance ghostwriting. I know how easy it is to think that ghostwriting is just another form of writing; in actuality, it has many subtle and not so subtle differences.

WHAT IS A GHOSTWRITING PROJECT?

Ghostwriting is simply defined as writing a book, or a shorter work, for someone else; we will refer to that person as the client. For the purposes of this discussion, we will focus on producing a book, but the same concepts can be applied to smaller works as well. The main difference between standard freelance writing and ghostwriting is that a ghostwriter does not receive credit for the book, nor are they listed as the author. Most of the concepts described in within this manuscript apply equally to a normal, non-ghostwritten, freelance book project.

Your job as a ghostwriter is to take the ideas and concepts of another person or persons and create a manuscript. You will not receive credit as the author. In most cases, you will not be listed in any way anywhere in the book.

There is more to ghostwriting than just creating a book. You are managing a project, and if you think of it that way you will have a greater chance of success.

On the other hand, if you think of ghostwriting as just interviewing and sitting down to write the next chapter, you probably will not be as successful. On those occasions where I have done this, I often found myself stuck in "revision hell."

I'm always excited to get new business. There's something about the thrill of that handshake that says, "I'm trusting you to write my book." It's very tempting to rush right in and start pounding the keys to create that first chapter or two. It seems like the right thing to do: to deliver some words on paper right away to prove that you are worthy of your client's trust.

Resist this tendency. Your client will feel better about you if you communicate well and often, and if you maintain control of the project. Delivering and agreeing to good outlines before writing a single word is far more important than rushing a chapter just to attempt to please your client. Agreeing on a good Statement of Work, well thought out agendas, interview protocol, and a solid change control process will ensure that you produce the best possible manuscript.

A SUCCESSFUL GHOSTWRITING PROJECT

To ensure your ghostwriting project is successful, keep it under control. Unless you are working for somebody else, you're in charge. Your client is depending on you to produce the best possible manuscript. In order to accomplish this, you need to use good project management skills from beginning to end.

Begin with communication. You must communicate with your client often, both orally and in writing. Remember, you're putting their story to words, and presumably it's important to them. By communicating often, you let your client know that the book is also important to you.

You must create a good Statement of Work (SOW) before you write a single word of the manuscript. The SOW's objective is to define the product, a book, as well as the process you will use to do the work. In addition, the contractual framework is established and agreed upon by all parties.

Change control is vital. Ghostwriting projects have a particular tendency to shift around as time unfolds. Your client may change his or her mind, the message may diversify or be altered, whole new chapters can be added, and any number of other things could happen as the book is written.

If you don't maintain control of change, your project can spin into disaster. Worse yet, you may wind up with a completed manuscript that the customer doesn't want, causing you to lose money. Nobody wins in that scenario.

One of the more important skills that you will use over and over again is outlining. No chapter should be written until a detailed outline is created and agreed upon by the client. It is much easier to change an outline than a fully written chapter.

AGREEMENT

The most vital component of any ghostwriting project is agreement. Do not proceed to the next step in the process until you get agreement from your client.

For example, at the start of the project create an SOW defining the structure, goals, and constraints. Before you write a chapter, you and your client must agree on an outline, and as you revise the book, your client must agree on those revisions.

At every step of the way, you must communicate with your client and get their agreement before moving forward. If you don't take the time to get that agreement, you are setting yourself up for extra revisions at the very least and a disaster at worst.

BRANDING

Include your branding on every communication that you send. Documents such as agendas, Statements of Work, and notes should be sent on your letterhead as an attachment to an email message. Create and use a branded email signature.

There are examples of branded documents later in this book. If you have developed a logo, include it on everything written.

Always put your company name and contact information on everything you put in front of the client. This is best done with an email signature and company letterhead. You don't want your client stumbling around trying to find your phone number or other ways to contact you. Put your contact information on all documents so it is always available to them.

IT IS A BUSINESS

Keep in mind that ghostwriting is a business. This is true even though you may be doing your writing at home, you are paid cash, or you haven't made very much money. Be professional at all times.

Many localities require a permit to work at home. You can usually find out what's needed by looking at the local

Chamber of Commerce website or making a visit to city hall. Do not neglect to get any permits needed for your business.

Keep good records of your income and expenses. Sometimes all that is necessary is a thorough spreadsheet or some simple bookkeeping software. I highly recommend, at the very least, that your taxes be done by a professional accountant.

You are self-employed if you are a freelance ghostwriter, which means you may need to pay self-employment tax to the IRS. Check with your accountant or a tax attorney for the details.

Track all expenses related to your business, as these can be used to reduce the amount of tax you owe. Anything you do for your business is generally deductible. Discuss this with your accountant.

Ensure you receive all your 1099s from each person that paid you more than $600 throughout the year. Report all income to the IRS, including any cash you received "under the table".

Communication is key

During a career spanning 35 years, I have found that communication is the key to completing any project successfully. Bad communication, or a lack of it entirely, has destroyed more projects than I care to remember. On the other hand, the common denominator of success is a habit of creating and maintaining a good connection between my team, the clients, and me.

A ghostwriting project is not an exception to this rule. In fact, communication is even more important in this realm of writing. The job of a ghostwriter is to take the ideas and concepts out of a person's mind and translate them into written words. You can only accomplish this with communication.

While you can talk via phone or Skype, you still need to record everything in writing and get the agreement of your client. To repeat, every step of a ghostwriting process requires the approval of the client; each time you fail to get approval, you risk having to go backward for revisions.

CONSTANT COMMUNICATIONS

You should make it a habit to communicate constantly, not randomly. From the first contact with your client, you need to maintain a steady stream of emails and documents. Obviously, you don't want to overwhelm them, but it is important to be communicating on a regular basis.

I recommend using email as a general rule. Unlike the phone, email is nonintrusive and can be read at your convenience. Also, emails can be saved, filed, forwarded, and referred to at a later date. Phone conversations do not have this advantage.

The time to start communicating is as early as the first discussion with your prospective client. Once you have their contact information, send them an email thanking them for their time and briefly describing your conversation.

After every phone conversation, send an email to your client overviewing the discussion. Document any and all understandings. Outline all decisions as bullet points. Your client can review these emails and respond if they have comments or disagreements.

When you receive documents, emails, checks, or anything else from your client, send an email acknowledging the receipt. If you have any disagreements, note that in the email.

By doing this, you will dramatically improve the chances of successfully completing your ghostwriting project. Your client will always know the current status of your work, and you will have a record of all decisions, understandings, and agreements throughout the project.

TYPES OF COMMUNICATION

I find that email is good for normal, day-to-day use. Most decisions and communications don't require an instant response; many can wait a few hours, or even a day or more. Using email for routine messages is more respectful of a person's time, as they can answer the message at their convenience.

Use the phone for interviews, quick decisions, and general discussions. Tools such as Skype are also valuable for these purposes.

When possible, nothing beats meeting in person. Two or more people can sit across from each other, talking, arguing, discussing, waving their arms, writing on whiteboards, and pacing while they talk, yet they can quickly turn ideas and concepts into usable outlines and manuscripts.

Remember, you are a professional writer. All communications, regardless of the form—email, document, agenda, quick note, or anything else in writing—must be spell checked and proofed for grammar. Nothing screams unprofessional more than spelling and grammar errors.

EMAIL MESSAGES

Be aware that, because email is faceless, unintended emotions can be communicated. Tersely worded phrases can say things you didn't intend. Not responding or acknowledging is often as a sign of disrespect. Humor can be grossly misinterpreted without body language available to read. Also, note that email messages can be read by others, who may not understand that you were joking. Make sure your messages are professional and avoid joking around.

Here is an example of a poorly worded email message:

Agreed.

Introduction

This is the same message, reworded in a professional manner:

Thank you for your comments. I agree with everything you've stated and will modify the manuscript as you requested.

Sincerely,
Richard G Lowe Jr.

It only takes a few more seconds to write a polite, professional response. Spend that time and avoid misunderstandings.

You should take the time to reinforce your branding by creating a good email signature. This adds an additional touch of professionalism to every email you send. Don't clutter up the signature with advertisements, and keep it to just a few lines. My email signature is shown below as an example.

Richard Lowe, CEO and Senior Writer
The Writing King. www.thewritingking.com - 966-653-4230 - rich@thewritingking.com
Author of "Real World Survival"

AGENDAS

All meetings and interviews must have an agenda. I've learned this the hard way after many years of managing small and large projects. A meeting without an agenda typically tends to go on for far too long while accomplishing very little.

An agenda is simply a bulleted list of discussion points for the meeting. Arrange it in order of importance, with the most critical point at the top and the least vital at the bottom. When you are in the meeting, start from the top and work down. That way if you run out of time, you can be sure that you've discussed the most important points first.

Occasionally, a meeting happens so quickly that you may not have time to create an agenda in advance. In this case, the first agenda item consists of creating the agenda. Do this before addressing any other business in the meeting. It only takes a few minutes to determine and record the discussion points.

Always write your agenda on your letterhead template. This reinforces your branding and provides all of your contact information to your client. Send it as an attachment to an email. An example of agenda written on my company letterhead follows.

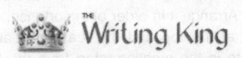

Agenda

Phone meeting, scheduled for July 2, 2015: 3:00pm EST

Topics to be discussed, not necessarily in order. Meeting should be an hour or less long.

- Restate and clarify the purpose and goal of the book.
- Go over notes
- Define the intended audience
- Discuss writing style
- Conclude with next meeting time and deliverables between now and then

~Page 1 ~

Richard Lowe • 340 South Lemon Avenue #5029, Walnut, CA 91789
866-653-4230• www.thewritingking.com • rich@thewritingking.com

NOTES

The Google Chromebook® is an excellent, inexpensive computer, and it is perfect for taking notes during meetings. When connected to Google Drive®, the notes are stored in the Cloud and may be accessed from anywhere.

Type your notes as the meeting progresses. Never have a meeting without taking notes. Make sure to record the following:

- ➤ Any decisions made
- ➤ Any decisions which were not made, along with any information needed
- ➤ Understandings between you and your client
- ➤ Any agreed-upon dates or dollar amounts and who made the agreement

➢ Any disagreements

There is an extension to Google Chrome® called Mic Note. This handy application uses the built-in mic of a laptop or tablet to record the sounds in the room. As it is recording your notes, the application includes a timestamp alongside the text. I have found this tool to be invaluable since it links my scribblings with the audio recording of the meeting.

If you use this kind of application, be sure to get the permission of everyone in the room before recording. This is a legal requirement. I make it a point to record the act of asking and receiving permission at the start of the meeting. This ensures there can be no doubt that permission was given.

Once the meeting is finished, using your agenda as a base to create a document of meeting notes. Make a copy of the agenda, and under each agenda item, include the decisions, understandings, and other applicable data. Use your letterhead for these notes.

Once you've proofread and spell-checked your notes, send them off to the client as an attachment to an email. Your client should never see your handwritten or draft notes.

REGULAR STATUS UPDATES

Once the project gets going, you may find that there are long stretches of time when you don't need to communicate with your client. Sometimes several days, a week, or longer can go by without requiring any meetings or decisions. Regardless, send regular status reports.

Introduction

Your client will appreciate receiving a short status report. Often, all you need to do is write a few lines in an email stating that you are making good progress. At other times, you might want to list articles you read for research, people you have interviewed, or other things you have done on the project. Make sure not to pester your client with too much data; it can be a fine line between communicating well and being overwhelming.

By maintaining a regular line of communication between you and your client, you ensure your project runs smoothly. There will be fewer misunderstandings, and you will be able to quickly work through any setbacks that may occur.

Getting the business

Where do ghostwriting projects come from in the first place? When I began, it was a mystery. How the heck do you find people who want a book written for them? How many people actually have the money to fund one of these projects?

A ghostwriting project can come from anywhere, at any time. I've landed books directly from contacts on LinkedIn®, from networking meetings, from friends, and from referrals. Sometimes they land in your lap seemingly out of the blue, and other times it requires weeks or even months of discussions and conversations to get the project started.

To be successful as a ghostwriter, you have to make yourself known. One good place to start is social networking sites, such as the following:

- ➤ **LinkedIn** – This is probably the best place on the web to begin your marketing adventures. LinkedIn is for business, which makes it a great source for new ghostwriting jobs.
- ➤ **Facebook®** – It's important to have a presence on Facebook, but I haven't found it to be very useful in generating leads. Create a Facebook page just for your business and promote it directly, but don't expect a wealth of business as a result.
- ➤ **Google+®** – As with Facebook, you should create a Google+ page for your business, but not expect a large return.
- ➤ **Your blog** – Creating and maintaining a blog is a lot of work. I know this from hard experience. It is

essential, however because you need a space on the web where people can go to find out more about you and your business. Make sure your blog looks professional, that it is updated regularly, and that there are no errors. Also, make sure the loading time of your blog is fast; web pages that take a long time to download chase away customers.

➤ **Other people's blogs** – You can write guest articles on other people's blogs that promote your business. Sometimes you can work out an exchange, pay a few dollars, or swap a favor and have your article included on their site in return.

➤ **Other networking sites** – There a number of other social networking sites on the web. Find those that are important to your niche, but be careful; it's easy to spend an inordinate amount of time playing on social networks instead of getting new business and writing.

In your local area, there are many ways you can network more directly. These include:

➤ Writers critique groups
➤ Meetup groups
➤ Libraries
➤ Groups that specialize in networking
➤ Technical users groups
➤ Anywhere else businesspeople or just people congregate

Join every writing critique group that you can find. These help you hone your writing skills and form bonds with other writers. These writers can also be a great source of referrals.

Join your local Chamber of Commerce and attend the meetings. Contribute and make it known that you are a ghostwriter. Make sure to explain in simple terms what a ghostwriter does as the job may be unfamiliar to some.

I could go on, but the basic concept is to find those groups, whether on the Internet or in person, and make yourself known to them. Communicate on a regular basis, and let them know how you can help. More important, keep your eyes and ears open for any hints of writing possibilities. You'd be amazed by the number of people who want to write a book but lack the time or skills to do so.

To land new business, you need to be getting yourself out there into the world. It's that simple. You won't gain any business if you don't let people know what you can do for them.

How much to charge

When I first started ghostwriting, I was paid around a thousand dollars to write a 20,000-word book. That included an initial interview during which an outline was created, eight chapters, eight more interviews, and revisions on the manuscript until the client accepted it.

That was a flat rate project, and I think when all was said and done, I wound up making about seven dollars an hour. I learned many important lessons from that experience, the most vital of which were not to underbid a project and to take into account everything that goes into ghostwriting.

The problem with ghostwriting, and with any type of project for that matter, is that a client always wants to know what it's going to cost up front. Generally, after one or two hours of conversation, at the most, questions concerning cost inevitably arise.

This places you in the situation of needing to name a price without enough information to give an accurate estimate. A potential client is usually not going to jump into a ghostwriting project without some idea of the cost.

Some ghostwriters work on a time-and-materials basis, charging their hourly rate for their time. I have yet to find a single client who will agree to this formula.

I structure ghostwriting projects into multiple phases. The first phase includes writing the first two chapters—each of which is between 2,000 and 3,000 words long—4 to 6 interviews, and 2 to 4 revisions for each chapter. Tasks such as outlining, emailing, writing agendas, and other overhead items are included in the estimate.

Thus, after the first one to a two-hour conversation with the client, where they describe what they want, I present them with a ballpark figure. I make it clear that that we will reevaluate the project cost after the first phase is complete, and this is clearly stated in the SOW.

Each phase is paid for in advance, and the first one is no exception.

By the end of the first phase, I have a good grasp of how the rest of the project is going to go. After half a dozen interviews, I know how easy or difficult the remaining ones will be. When the first two chapters are complete, I have a good idea of how long it will take to write each of the remaining ones. The overall style, point of view, and intended audience are also determined by the end of the first phase.

Upon finishing that work, I take another look at the rest of the project and determine if my original estimate was correct. If I believe the book will require more or less work than I originally thought, I discuss it with the client and get approval for the change in cost. There may be some negotiation involved, but generally, if you have all the facts, the client will agree. Of course, they may decide they don't want to pay the additional expense, and the book might end right there. In any event, the amount paid for in the first phase is not refunded.

This process is written directly into the SOW, and must be stressed to the client on several occasions. You never want this to be a surprise to your client.

This technique is advantageous for both the client and the ghostwriter. It gives the client an initial ballpark figure so they can make a decision as to whether or not to proceed with the project. It protects the ghostwriter by allowing room to renegotiate costs if the project turns out to be more difficult than initially thought. If the new price is not acceptable by both parties, the client and ghostwriter can part ways amicably.

Building in this first phase resolves the conundrum of all ghostwriting projects. The client must have an idea of how much the book is going to cost before he can justify funding it. I, on the other hand, don't have enough information to give the client a solid estimate, and this can easily turn into a catch 22 situation.

PRICING FORMULA

The basic formula for pricing a ghostwriting project begins with your hourly rate. For example, if you charge $20 an hour, then the cost of the project is based on that. Estimate how many interviews you need, how long each will be, how much research needs to be done, how many revisions you will allow, how much overhead there is, and any other work you need to do.

You can create a spreadsheet that includes each task required to complete a phase of the project. Include columns for the quantity of each task, hours required for each task, your hourly rate, and the total cost per task. Add it all up, plus a percentage as contingency, and you have an estimate.

The following spreadsheet shows how to do this. Note that this is simplified for illustration purposes. You may have more or fewer line items depending on your project.

Task	Qty	Hours	Rate	Cost
Interviews	6	1	$20.00	$120.00
Research	8	1	$20.00	$160.00
Writing 2 chapters	16	1	$20.00	$320.00
Meetings	2	1	$20.00	$40.00
Overhead	4	1	$20.00	$80.00
	TOTAL			$720.00
	CONTINGINCY			$288.00
	TOTAL ESTIMATE			$1,008.00

If the project involves traveling, include estimates for that in your price as well. For the time you spent driving or flying, your hourly rate applies. After all, your time is worth money. Some clients will want to negotiate this out of the SOW; use your best judgment. If you charge hours for traveling, do not charge mileage. If the client does not pay your hourly rate for driving, charge for mileage at the standard IRS rate.

Also include expenses you expect to incur. Your SOW should specify that expenses are be approved by and billed back to the client. Bill them at your cost. Don't include a markup.

The key to making this process work is to make sure you do a good job on the first phase. You also need to carefully control changes to the scope of the project.

Obviously, there is some risk that the first phase may require more effort than you initially believed. Adding 30% to 40% contingency can help with that. I have found that my estimates of the first phase are generally accurate, but on those occasions when it took me longer to complete than I expected, I absorbed the cost.

However, changes in scope requiring additional work add extra cost to the project. Your SOW should detail the hours allocated to the first phase. For example, one of my contracts states there will be six interviews, eight hours of research, two chapters of about 3,000 words each, plus up to four revisions of each of those two chapters. From that it was possible for me to make a reasonable estimate of what the first phase would cost.

I no longer make the mistake of fixed bidding the whole project up front. It is not possible to fully grasp what goes into a book after just an hour or two of conversation with a client. You have to build in some flexibility, and that is done with a proper SOW that allows the project to be reevaluated after the initial analysis is complete.

Statement of work

The most important thing you can do for ghostwriting success is write and obtain the client's agreement on a comprehensive Statement of Work (SOW). The client should always sign the SOW before you begin the project.

An SOW is a contractual agreement between two or more parties. This document defines the scope of the project and the working relationship between all involved. It includes payment terms, milestones, and other things pertinent to the project, such as:

- The estimated total cost, clearly stating it is an estimate
- How and when to make payments for services
- How expenses are to be handled
- Termination clauses
- Ownership of the manuscript, notes, interviews, and so on
- Confidentiality
- A rough description of the product to be delivered
- Estimated word count, the number of chapters, etc.
- Estimated research required
- The number of revisions allowed
- Services not included, such as proofreading or cover art
- The responsibilities of each party
- Phases and deliverables for each phase
- An arbitration paragraph
- A request for an acknowledgment for writing the book

THE BASICS

As we discussed in the previous section, it is difficult to estimate the total cost and length of a project based upon one or two conversations with a prospective client. Nonetheless, the client requires some kind of figure before approving the project. In my SOWs, I like to define the first phase as an exploratory period to determine the actual cost and size of the remainder of the work.

I find that 25% of the total estimated cost is enough to cover this exploratory and analysis phase. The SOW should clearly state that you will revisit the original estimate for the project at the end of the first phase, as the scope and price may change. The price may go up or down depending upon what was discovered during the first phase.

For ghostwriting, payments need to be made in advance of work. By splitting the project into phases, this becomes agreeable to most clients. Do not start the project without advance payment; the SOW needs to spell that out explicitly.

Also, payments are non-refundable. By splitting the project up into multiple phases, this becomes palatable to the client.

TERMINATION

You must include a termination clause in your SOW. This grants either party the right to terminate the project before starting any phase. The SOW should make it clear that prior payments will not be refunded in the event of termination. After all, the work has already been done and delivered.

Whether the project completes successfully or not, all materials must be returned to the client. You must deliver any notes, interviews, recordings, unfinished or finished manuscripts, and everything else related to the book at that time.

Remember, you're being paid in advance for work performed. Therefore, you have an obligation to deliver to your client any work you've done upon termination or successful conclusion.

COPYRIGHT

Since you are engaging in a ghostwriting project, the SOW needs to make it clear that you are doing it on a work for hire basis. State explicitly that all copyrights for the manuscript, whether completed or not, belong to the client.

MULTIPLE PHASES

Spell out each part of the project, beginning with the first phase, which we went over at length earlier in this book.

Loosely define the remaining phases in the SOW. Include language explaining that you will further define these phases after the first one is complete.

The deliverables for the first phase should be very detailed. Explain in your SOW that you'll be doing analysis, interviews, research (if applicable), and so forth. I like to include writing the first and second chapters of the book in the first phase so that the voice, formality, and style are worked out before proceeding to later phases.

Also, my SOWs allow extra revisions for the first two chapters to give my client and me the ability to go back and forth several times until we have it right.

SERVICES NOT INCLUDED

Be sure to list the services that you do not include in the project. I typically don't offer the following:

- ➤ Professional proofreading and copy editing
- ➤ Book cover
- ➤ Publishing
- ➤ Marketing
- ➤ Graphics
- ➤ Formatting required for publication

Proofreading, for example, should be done by a professional trained in that skill. Book covers need to be designed by someone who does that well. The job of a ghostwriter is to write, and I've found it better to stick to what I do best.

On those occasions where I offered these services to a client, I did so under a separate and distinct SOW.

ACKNOWLEDGMENTS

One of the frustrating things about being a ghostwriter is the difficulty of creating a portfolio. The book, after all, names your client as the author. In fact, in most cases you are not acknowledged as having anything to do with the manuscript.

In my SOWs, I include a paragraph that requests recognition in the *Acknowledgments* section of the manuscript. I word it as a request, and it is entirely optional to the client. Nonetheless, no one has objected yet.

Writing the book

Now it's time to get down to the nitty-gritty of writing the book. Well, actually, there are a few steps you need to do before you sit down and start pounding on the keyboard.

First, you'll need to do some interviews, and probably some research. For a typical nonfiction book, I've found that two interviews per chapter are more than enough. Simple chapters may require one interview while more complex ones require three or four.

Many books need research to get the facts, to validate what was said during an interview, or to find some statistics or quotes. Including quotes and statistics from other sources lends credibility to your manuscript.

Before you write a single chapter, outline it fully and completely. A typical outline for a chapter may have 3 to 10 major bullet points, and each bullet point might include anywhere from three to a dozen sub-points. The major bullet points become subheadings, and the sub-points work out to one or two paragraphs each.

This outline is an agreement between you and your client that defines the chapter. Once you've got an understanding, you can begin writing. Ideally, you get that agreement, at least orally, by the end of the final interview for the chapter.

Send your outline to the client for a more formal approval. An acknowledgment via email is fine. At this point, go ahead and start writing the chapter. Sometimes the client will send the outline back with changes, but they are almost never significant.

Once you've gone through this process for a chapter, move on to the next one. Continue doing this until you have a finished book.

PARTS OF A BOOK

Before jumping into explaining how to ghostwrite a manuscript, let's briefly look at each of the parts of a book. Your SOW should define which of these is your responsibility, and which the client needs to handle. For example, in most of the books I've ghostwritten, the client handles the foreword, as this is written by authority figures to provide background on the author or the book.

Just make sure that your statement of work defines clearly says who handles each of the sections.

> **Title page**. The title page includes the title of the book, the subtitle, the author's name, and quite often the address of a website.
> **Dedication page**. On this page, your client can dedicate the book to a person or group.
> **Acknowledgments**. A short section where the author (your client) acknowledges those who were in some way helpful.
> **Table of contents**. A list of the chapters and subchapters in the book. Modern word processors can create this automatically, as long as you use styles to define your headings.

- ➢ **Forward**. One or more essays that are written by other people providing background to the book and the author.
- ➢ **Preface**. Important information related to the book or the author.
- ➢ **Introduction**. Introduces the book, typically intended to build excitement. Include a hook to get the reader to want to continue.
- ➢ **Body**. The main text of the manuscript, which is broken up into chapters.
- ➢ **Afterward**. An optional section that gives any additional data the reader might need to know after finishing the book.
- ➢ **Glossary**. Define any of the words specific to the subject.
- ➢ **Bibliography**. This section lists any references used in writing the book. A citation style, such as MLA or Chicago, is often used for consistency.
- ➢ **Index**. An alphabetical list of topics discussed in the book. You do not want to index every occurrence of a word or topic. Only index those that the reader is likely to reference.
- ➢ **Author biography**. A brief, generally no more than single page section about the author. This is written in the third person.

The order of these sections is different in eBooks than in books intended for hardcopy distribution. In an eBook, most of the front material is moved to the back so that the *Look Inside* feature offered by some distributors shows more useful information to help attract buyers.

PREREQUISITES

Before you begin writing your book, create a folder on your computer or cloud service in which to store all documents related to the manuscript. By doing this, you will make it easy to keep the project organized. Create subfolders as needed for further organization.

Create templates and put those into a templates subfolder. All documents should be created based on these templates.

Use styles to make formatting changes easier down the road. Your styles are defined as part of your templates.

Obviously, you need to choose the word processor you are going to use. Ensure that your word processor is compatible with the one used by your client.

INTERVIEWS

For each chapter of the book, you should plan on doing one or more interviews. I usually perform two interviews per chapter with each chapter being between 2,000 and 3,000 words.

I like to record each interview. If you do this, be sure to inform the client that he or she is being recorded at the start of the interview. There are applications for phones that will record calls. A tablet or a Google Chromebook® is ideal for interviews because you can record and type notes at the same time

Send an agenda for the interview in advance. This gives your client time to think about the answers to your questions and do any research necessary.

At the start of the interview, the first thing to do is to define the purpose of the chapter. What does the client want the reader to know and to feel by the end?

Define each of your questions as bullet points on an agenda. You may find as you go through the interview that additional points need to be addressed. Simply add those to the agenda.

One of the skills you need is the ability remain on track. One technique is to define in advance how long the interview will last. If your client gets too far off track, you can point to your watch and use that to get them back to the task at hand.

Of course, remain polite at all times. Maintain control of the interview, get your questions answered, and understand the voice and point of view of your client.

Before the interview is over, define the hook that causes the reader to want to go on to the next chapter. When your outline is complete and agreed upon by the client, you are ready to start writing.

RESEARCH

One of the very first ghostwriting projects that I did required a significant amount of research before writing could begin. The book was a memoir of a person from another country. I had to research the history of his country, the culture, and the religious context of the area.

It was frustrating, as the contract did not include research of that magnitude. Since the project was fixed-price, I lost money on the deal. The lesson that I learned is to ensure that the SOW includes a limit on the number of research hours to be provided.

Sometimes you will find that you need to research as you write, which is normal for a ghostwriting project. Just do what you need to do.

Wikipedia is not a reliable source for most information. The data within can be edited by anyone and should never be used as a primary source.

OUTLINE EACH CHAPTER

Through experience, I have learned that simply jumping in and writing each chapter immediately after an interview doesn't work very well. I have found it is better to create a detailed outline during the interview process. Working together, the client and I define each point to be addressed. The goal is to have a chapter outline complete and agreed upon by the end of the last interview for the chapter.

The completed outline defines the scope of work for the chapter. While this might seem like a lot of extra work, it eliminates revisions down the line. The basic concept is to obtain agreement from your client that ensures what you intend to write is what the client wants in the chapter.

DOING THE WRITING

Once you and your client have completed the outline, it is time to begin writing the chapter. Set aside a block of time, whatever works best for you, and write. Personally, I find like to bang out a whole chapter in one shot. For some people that works. Others prefer to write in small chunks. Do whatever works for you.

Once you've finished writing the chapter, set it aside and do something else for a few hours. Better yet, put it away until the next day, then pick up the chapter and read it from start to finish cut. Correct any errors that you find and revise as needed.

As an extra precaution, take the time to read the chapter again from front to back out loud. You'd be amazed how many errors you can find by doing this step.

I use a tool called Grammarly® to double check my grammar. There are other tools that perform similar functions. These are very useful to ensure your manuscript is of high quality.

Never deliver anything to your client that contains spelling errors. Use the spell checking option of your editor. Correct any errors before sending anything to your client.

REVISIONS

Once you finish your chapter, and you have proofread it to make sure there are no spelling errors, email it to your client. Turn on tracking, so that you can identify any changes they make.

In the email message that accompanies the chapter, detail any questions you may have, anything you want your client to focus on, and when you'd like the revisions returned to you.

At this point, there will be a short delay as your client reviews the chapter. If you don't get it back with revisions in the timeframe you expect, send an email to ask for status, but don't overwhelm them. You can always make a phone call if your client is running very late.

Once you get the revisions back examine them and make the changes as needed. Most of the time, assuming you have a good outline, the revisions will be relatively minor. This is normal editing and won't change the scope of the work.

Sometimes your client will request a significant change. As long as the change is limited in scope to the current chapter, I'll make the revisions as requested.

It is quite common for a chapter to go back and forth between you and the client a couple of times.

When the client accepts the chapter, go ahead and proceed to the next one. As before, start with the interviews and outlines before writing. Sometimes you can overlap the revising of a chapter with the interviewing of the next chapter. Use your best judgment depending upon the subject material and the client's working style.

AFTER THE CHAPTER IS ACCEPTED

Once you've gone through one or more revisions, the chapter should be looking pretty good. Get the client to agree it is complete. An email is acceptable for this purpose.

If your outline is good, if your proofreading was top-notch, and if you have no spelling errors, your revisions should be quick and easy. You can use the revision limits in your SOW to limit the number of changes so you can move forward with the next chapter. With a good outline, however, this is rarely needed.

Once the client approves a chapter, no further changes can be made without going through change control. Evaluate any changes to estimate how much work is required. Once you have an estimate, decide if there is additional cost involved.

Don't get me wrong, there will be changes to earlier chapters, even if only due to grammar or spelling errors. Turn on tracking, make any changes, and then send it to your client for approval. After that, this becomes the new baseline.

Make sure anytime you send a chapter to the client that tracking is turned on. That way you can see what was changed.

Major Revisions

There are always changes as a ghostwriting project proceeds. It's a normal part of the game, and you shouldn't be alarmed by it. Make sure your client understands this up front to prevent misunderstandings later.

The process outlined in this book is designed to reduce the possibility of needing to go backward to make revisions. The idea is to gain your client's approval as you proceed rather than waiting until the end. You do this by

> ➢ Creating a solid statement of work
> ➢ Providing an overall outline for the entire book
> ➢ Creating and agreeing to an outline before writing each chapter
> ➢ Revising each chapter with your client as you go
> ➢ Keeping a log of changes

Since you are getting an agreement at each step of the way, it becomes more and more unlikely the client will want to change earlier material.

The most common reason for major changes to occur happens when the client sends the unfinished manuscript to others for review. Watch out for this, as it is a hidden landmine threatening to explode and damage the scope of your project beyond recognition. If an earlier chapter comes back to you with major changes, this is the most likely reason.

Introduction

Understand the difference between minor revisions and changes to the point of view, structure, or overall feel of the manuscript. Major changes may require additional costs if they take significant time to address.

LOG CHANGES

I maintain a spreadsheet of any changes as I proceed through the project.

Date	Change	Requested by	Chapter	Date approved	Cost
7/1/2015	Rewrite introduction	Bill	1	7/2/2015	$0.00
7/2/2015	Change to 1st person, 2 chapters	Bill	1&2	7/3/2015	$400.00

Keep this simple. There is no need to add extra administration. This log is useful under many circumstances. For example, if your client questions you about the need to charge more for the book, you can use it to show all of the changes that have been approved with and without additional cost.

NO CHANGES ARE REQUESTED

Each week, many years ago, a client returned all of my chapters with no changes. I didn't think much about it at the time, as he included a note that said it looked good.

When I completed and delivered the book, I thought we were done. Unfortunately, my client had decided on his own that he wasn't going to review anything until the document was finished.

At that point, we went round and round making revision after revision of the entire manuscript.

This was a very expensive lesson, primarily because the revisions went all the way back to the first chapter. As a result, a straightforward one month project expanded to a three-month monster.

Make sure your SOW clearly says that when a chapter is approved, it's finished. Going back to earlier chapters is a change in scope that may add additional time and cost to the project. It is critically important for the manuscript to be reviewed chapter by chapter as it is written to prevent major rework down the road.

You will occasionally get a chapter back without any edits. That should be a very rare occurrence, and you'd be wise to discuss it with your client. Make sure they understand the importance of reviewing as the manuscript is written.

WATCH OUT FOR CHANGES IN SCOPE

Your Statement of Work must include verbiage that clearly states that changes in scope may require additional cost. A change might be as simple as one more interview than was anticipated, or as complex as the need to rewrite four chapters already completed and approved.

We'll get into changes in scope in the next chapter, but occasionally they will be buried in the document revisions requested by the client. There might be a comment that directs you to perform a major rewrite or change the point of view. Revisions are expected; however if the request causes a need to rewrite earlier chapters, then handle it as a change in scope and determine if you need to ask for additional money and time.

Changes in scope

As I've said before, it doesn't matter whether it's a small project or large one; there will be changes as the book unfolds. Change is inevitable in any project, and it's particularly likely in a ghostwriting scenario.

A key point to successfully ghostwriting a book is to keep changes under control. Do not get the idea that you must adjust the cost of the manuscript for every little modification; in fact, quite the opposite is true. The point of change control is to ensure a methodology is in place. Without this process, you are setting yourself up for failure.

Your SOW should include a statement of how to manage change, beginning with simple changes. For example, I wouldn't increase the project cost for minor revisions after reviewing the document, a request to add a few more paragraphs to the chapter completed last week, or even an extra interview that wasn't in the budget.

Save your cost adjustments for larger modifications, such as the addition of new chapters or going back and modifying the point of view of the entire book.

Be sure you log any changes in scope as you proceed. Do not try and make this up later from memory.

MINOR SCOPE CHANGES

As each chapter is outlined and written, revisions are normal and expected. Don't handle these as changes in scope. These are simply a part of writing a chapter.

However, there are times when the customer requests changes that alter the basic outline of a chapter after it has been written, revised, and approved. In these instances, review your budget and your SOW to determine if an adjustment in the price is needed.

Treat this area with care. The manuscript will naturally change as you interview your client, produce outlines and have the client read the first draft of the chapter. Make sure your estimates for the project include sufficient time for this type of revision. You do not want to give the impression of nickel and diming them to death. No one likes that.

If you do determine that a change is more than just a revision but doesn't require any additional money or time, just record that fact in an email, send it off to your client, and note it in your log. Keep the communication flowing, and be sure to tell him whether or not there is additional cost or time involved.

CHANGES THAT RESULT IN HIGHER COST

There will be instances where you need to ask your client for more money. For example, this can happen if your client asks for additional chapters, or you need to go back and change the point of view throughout the whole book.

I worked on one book where the client had reviewed, revised, and approved eight of the twelve chapters. He decided he wanted the whole thing changed to first person, even though he had previously agreed to a third person point of view. If this happens, you need to decide if additional costs are required. In this case, I decided to absorb the costs since there was room in the budget.

Ensure that any increases in cost or that result in changes to the schedule are documented in writing and signed by your client. Get a written agreement for any change that costs extra money. Don't just add it to the next invoice, hoping you can slip it by. This is unethical behavior, and it will catch up to you later.

CHANGES THAT REQUIRE EXPENSES

Occasionally, a change might require additional expenses. For example, your client might identify an additional person to interview who was not originally included in the SOW. If you have to meet them in person, you should be compensated for the expenses.

Always communicate with your client and get an agreement before incurring any expenses. Never bill expenses that have not been approved in advance by the client.

REVISITING PREVIOUSLY COMPLETED WORK

I worked on one project where we got five chapters into a 10 to 12 chapter book, which was about 25,000 words. The client sent the manuscript to his daughter, and she didn't agree with the structure of the book.

The client had reviewed all five chapters, revised them extensively, and had agreed they were complete and acceptable. Going back to revise those five chapters would require significant time. Thus, asking for more money was justified.

Remember to use your discretion when deciding whether or not to absorb the additional costs and time of significant changes. Someone is going to absorb the cost; if you don't charge extra you absorbed it. If you charge extra, the client pays the cost. Sometimes, of course, you can negotiate and split the difference down the middle. It all depends on the situation.

ALL SCOPE CHANGES DOCUMENTED IN WRITING
I have said this several times already, but make sure you document any scope changes in writing and in a log.

Document standard revisions using change tracking within your favorite word processor. Send the document to the client with revision tracking turned on. Any changes made by the client will be noted. Once you receive the revised document, use revision control to see the modifications. Save this document; that is your record of the revisions.

Document changes to the scope that are more significant but don't require additional money or time via an exchange of emails. Do not make any changes without approval from your client. The exchange of email serves as this approval.

If the client doesn't return an email accepting or acknowledging the change request, add it to your agenda for the next interview or meeting. You can get approval, or disapproval, at that time. Of course, you can always make a phone call if the client is not returning your email. After the call, be sure to send an email documenting what was decided.

Final revision

Once you've completed writing all of the chapters and the front and back material, you're in the final revision stage. Typically, the last thing to be approved is the front and back matter.

If you managed the project tightly, kept changes under control, maintained good communication with the client, and got the approval of each chapter as you proceeded, the final revision stage should be very straightforward.

This is because you've already received approval for everything. Now you're putting it together into a finished package and getting the final okay on the entire manuscript.

There will be some revisions requested at this stage. That's normal and expected. You should appropriate a few hours in your estimates to handle this.

In my experience, the most significant revisions occur after the client sends the book out for somebody else to review. This normally happens at this phase of the project. The revisions that come back at this point can be quite significant; this is often the touchiest part of ghostwriting. The client has requested significant changes to a book that you believed was finished.

Start by evaluating the changes. I wrote one book and sent it to the client at the end of the project. We had been communicating well throughout and I believed there would only be a few minor adjustments. However, the client sent

Introduction

the manuscript to a friend, who suggested hundreds of changes.

At first, I was upset. After all, the client had approved everything up to this point. However, once I reviewed the changes, I realized they were mostly cosmetic, and I had the revisions integrated into the final document within a few hours.

You have to use your judgment at this point. You may need to have to have some conversations with the client, and negotiations may be in order.

Even though you've already been paid long before this stage of the project, don't fall into the trap of trying to rush through or avoid making those revisions. After all, we all want happy clients, good books, and referrals. Keep your cool, stay in communication with the client, and come to a reasonable agreement as to how to complete the book.

EDIT ENTIRE DOCUMENT

Before sending the book to the client during the final revision part of the project, read through the entire thing again. Read it from the first page to the last. Ensure there are no spelling or grammar errors.

You may find things that need to be corrected. Ensure you have turned on document tracking so that all changes are noted.

Completing the project

You finally reached the end of the project. Congratulations! Your hard work has paid off.

At this point, your client has signed off on the book. Ask them to sign a document that states the project is done and has been delivered.

Put together a package that includes final document and any supporting files, such as interviews or research notes.

Your SOW should spell out the deliverables upon completion. You can email these as a zip file, load them on a USB key, or write them to a DVD. Request an acknowledgment in writing—an email is fine—confirming everything was received and accepted.

REFERRAL AND TESTIMONIAL

Ask for referrals and ask the client to write a testimonial. These are important for you to use when soliciting future business.

Sometimes you can write a testimonial and send it to your client for their approval. It is best to ask before you do this. In my experience, most clients will use this as a starting point and modify it to be in their own words.

Always get a testimonial. Your name is not on the book; you are not going to become rich and famous from that manuscript. A testimonial is often the only evidence that you can use as proof of the work you accomplished. This is valuable, even though by the testimonial will often not include the name of the book.

REVISIONS AFTER COMPLETION

It is not uncommon for the book to come back to you a few weeks or even a few months later for some additional revisions. This often happens after the client will have friends, co-workers, peers, or their spouse read the book.

At this point, additional revisions can be done as a new project or as an addendum to the existing one. It's up to you, but you should ask for and receive additional compensation.

Conclusion

Ghostwriting is one of the most demanding forms of writing there is. You are not writing a book for your satisfaction; you're writing it for someone else.

To successfully pull off a ghostwriting project, you will need many skills beyond the ability to write. You need to know how to interview, run a meeting, create and stick to an estimate, handle changes in scope, and deal with the revision cycle.

You may find yourself doing quite a bit of negotiating as the project proceeds, especially when the scope of work changes. You may need to compromise on cost to make these changes. More than a few times I've split the difference, accepting half the estimate.

It is vital to keep your client on track throughout the project and during interviews. Sometimes there will be language barriers and accents that add an additional challenge.

Even so, ghostwriting can be one of the most fulfilling forms of writing there is. The sheer number of interviews needed may be enough to take you out of your comfort zone, but they also allow for opportunities to learn new things and explore different cultures and religions.

On the negative side, the books you write normally cannot be used in your portfolio. Typically, ghostwriting is anonymous. All of my ghostwriting contracts prohibit me from informing others that I am the author.

Thus, it is important for a ghostwriter to write and publish his or her own works. This is how you provide examples of your writing skills to future clients: publish some of your own books.

It is easy for a ghostwriting project to spin out of control; if changes are not properly managed you can lose money, the client can lose confidence in you, and your reputation can be damaged.

I trust this book will be of value in your new adventure. I hope you can put to use the techniques I've shared to help you successfully write and deliver ghostwritten books.

Before you go

If you scroll to the last page in this eBook, you will have the opportunity to leave feedback and share the book with Before You Go. I'd be grateful if you turned to the last page and shared it with your friends, coworkers, and family.

Also, if you have time, please leave a review. Positive reviews are incredibly useful. If you didn't like the book, please email me at rich@thewritingking.com and I'd be happy to get your input.

About the Author

https://www.linkedin.com/in/richardlowejr
Feel free to send a connection request

Follow me on Twitter: @richardlowejr

After spending over 33 years in the computer and information technology industry, Richard decided to take an early retirement to pursue his dreams of becoming a professional writer and published author. Richard is a leader in the computer industry, serving as Vice President of Consulting at Software Techniques and Beck Computer Systems before settling down as Director of Computer Operations at Trader Joe's. During his twenty-year tenure at that esteemed company, he focused on computer security, disaster recovery, warehouse logistics and retail merchandising.

Richard has published over 60 books under his own name, plus many more using various pseudonyms. His first two volumes, Safe Computing is Like Safe Sex and Real World Survival Tips and Survival Guide, respectively touch on the subjects of computer security and how to survive emergencies and disasters.

Richard has also written and published a series of short eBooks on the aspects of freelance writing, including blogging and ghostwriting. Other published books include How to Throw Parties Like a Professional and How to Be Friends with Women: How to Surround Yourself with

<u>Beautiful Women without Being Sleazy</u>. To see all the books he has available, visit:

http://www.coolauthor.com

In addition to creating hundreds of articles for the web and blogs, Richard actively works as a professional ghostwriter. In that role, he has completed books on a wide variety of subjects including memoirs, business volumes, and novels. Because of his in-depth background in software management and computer security, Richard has ghostwritten a number of major books in those areas.

A partial list of his freelance works includes:

- KnowBe4, a major computer security company, contracted with Richard to update the 2010 version of their book Cyberheist to include the threats of 2016.
- Ghostwrote a major book about the Internet of Things.
- Ghostwrote a major book about Artificial Intelligence.
- Ghostwrote a book about Retirement.
- Ghostwrote a book about Office Cleaning.
- Ghostwrote a book about Dentistry.
- Ghostwrote a book about Scrum and Agile.
- Ghostwrote a memoir of an Afghani politician.
- Ghostwrote a book about Sales.
- Ghostwrote a book about Property Management.
- Wrote a series of blog articles on the effect of technology on the trucking industry.
- Wrote a series of whitepapers about Augmented Reality.
- Wrote a series of blogs about HVAC.
- Wrote a series of blogs about Finances.

An avid adventurer, Richard has been a photographer for much of his life, with a focus on nature, scenic, performance and event photography. He has done everything from hiking in dozens of national parks throughout the country, to photographing various unique festivals and events, such as the Labyrinth of Jareth Masquerade Ball and the World Mermaid Awards Convention. He is well known in the Renaissance Festival and Belly Dance communities, having photographed over 1,200 dance events and 400 festivals.

Introduction

For several years, he photographed the Tournament of Roses Parade in Pasadena, California.

To help authors write, publish and promote their works, Richard teaches courses that are sold at Fiction Master Class. These are designed to help writers learn the skills they need to succeed.

Richard is rapidly writing short Kindle eBooks on a wide variety of fiction and nonfiction subjects. Beginning in 2018, the first of a ten-volume series of Science Fiction novels will be published.

One of Richard's passions is to use the power of words to educate people on human rights. He believes the world will be a better place when human beings are treated with the full respect and dignity they are due.

I've written and published many books on a variety of subjects. They are all listed on the following page.

https://www.richardlowe.guru

On that site, I also publish articles about business, writing, and other subjects. You can visit by clicking the following link:

https://www.thewritingking.com

To find out more about me or my photography, you can visit these sites:

Personal website: https://www.richardlowe.com
Photography: http://www.richardlowejr.com
Courses for fiction writers:
https://www.fictionmasterclass.com
LinkedIn Profile: https://www.linkedin.com/in/richardlowejr

If you have any comments about this book, feel free to email
me at rich@thewritingking.com

Made in United States
North Haven, CT
13 October 2023

42712367R10039